Chapter 1: Introduction

Welcome to "Essential Counterintelligence", a comprehensive guide to understanding and implementing counterintelligence techniques. In today's world, the threat of espionage, stalking, identity theft, and other forms of illicit information gathering is greater than ever. Whether it's state-sponsored actors, criminal organizations, or lone actors, the risks to national security and private enterprise are significant. That's why it's essential to have a robust and effective counterintelligence program in place.

In this book, we will explore the various techniques used in counterintelligence, from surveillance and undercover operations to technical surveillance and cyber counterintelligence. We will provide detailed instructions on how to implement these techniques and offer practical advice on developing and managing a successful counterintelligence program.

Whether you are a government agency, private business, or individual looking to protect your sensitive information, this book is a valuable resource. So let's dive in and learn how to protect ourselves and our organizations from the ever-present threat of espionage and other forms of illicit information gathering.

Chapter 2: Origins of Counterintelligence

Counterintelligence has a long and storied history, dating back to ancient times. The earliest known example of counterintelligence was in ancient Egypt, where pharaohs would use spies to gather information on their enemies and potential threats to their rule. The pharaohs also established a network of informants to keep an eye on the population and detect any signs of rebellion or dissent.

In ancient Greece, military commanders would use scouts and spies to gather information on the enemy's movements and intentions. The Spartans, in particular, were known for their use of intelligence gathering, which gave them a strategic advantage in many battles.

The Romans also had a sophisticated intelligence network, which included both military and civilian personnel. They used informants, double agents, and encrypted messages to gather and transmit information. The Romans were also known for their use of deception, such as creating fake documents or spreading false rumors, to mislead their enemies.

During the Middle Ages, counterintelligence was primarily used by monarchs and rulers to maintain their power and suppress dissent. The use of informants, surveillance, and secret police was widespread, particularly in authoritarian regimes.

It wasn't until the 20th century that counterintelligence began to take on its modern form. The First World War saw the establishment of intelligence agencies, such as the British MI6 and the American Office of Naval Intelligence. These agencies were tasked with gathering and analyzing information on the enemy's military capabilities and intentions.

The Second World War saw a significant expansion of intelligence gathering and counterintelligence operations, particularly by the Allies. The use of cryptography, such as the Enigma machine, allowed intelligence agencies to intercept and decipher enemy communications. The use of double agents, such as the famous "Cambridge Five", also proved to be a valuable tool in gathering intelligence on the enemy.

The Cold War period, which lasted from the late 1940s to the early 1990s, was a time of heightened tension between the Western powers led by the United States and the Soviet Union and their allies. The threat of nuclear war loomed large, and both sides engaged in extensive intelligence gathering and counterintelligence operations.

One of the most infamous incidents of the Cold War was the Cambridge spy ring, a group of British intelligence officers who passed information to the Soviet Union during the 1940s and 1950s. The spy ring included Kim Philby, Donald Maclean, Guy Burgess, and Anthony Blunt, all of whom had been recruited by the Soviet intelligence agency, the KGB. The revelation of the spy ring caused a major scandal in Britain and led to a crackdown on Communist sympathizers.

In the United States, the Federal Bureau of Investigation (FBI) and the Central Intelligence Agency (CIA) both played significant roles in counterintelligence during the Cold War era. The FBI's Counterintelligence Program, also known as COINTELPRO, was established in the 1950s to disrupt and neutralize political organizations deemed to be a threat to national security. The program was criticized for its use of illegal and unethical tactics, such as wiretapping and blackmail.

The CIA's counterintelligence efforts were focused on preventing Soviet and Communist infiltration of the agency itself. The agency established a number of counterintelligence units, including the Office of Security, which conducted background checks on potential employees, and the Counterintelligence Center, which investigated suspected moles within the agency.

The Cold War era was also marked by a number of high-profile spy cases, including the arrest and conviction of Julius and Ethel Rosenberg for passing nuclear secrets to the Soviet Union, and the defection of KGB agent Vitaly Yurchenko to the United States.

The collapse of the Soviet Union in the early 1990s marked a major shift in the global balance of power and had significant implications for counterintelligence. The end of the Cold War reduced the immediate threat of nuclear war and espionage, but it also created new challenges for intelligence agencies.

One of the main challenges faced by counterintelligence agencies in the post-Cold War era was the rise of non-state actors and terrorist groups. The 1993 World Trade Center bombing and the 1995 Oklahoma City bombing were both carried out by domestic terrorists, highlighting the need for intelligence agencies to shift their focus from traditional nation-state adversaries to non-state actors.

Another major challenge was the increasing use of technology in intelligence gathering and counterintelligence. The growth of the internet and the proliferation of mobile devices have made it easier for individuals and organizations to communicate and share information, but it has also created new vulnerabilities for counterintelligence agencies to exploit.

In response to these challenges, many intelligence agencies have adapted their tactics and strategies. The CIA, for example, has shifted its focus from traditional espionage to counterterrorism and cyber operations. The agency's Counterterrorism Center is responsible for coordinating intelligence and operational activities related to counterterrorism, while the Cyber Threat Intelligence Integration Center is focused on identifying and countering cyber threats.

Similarly, the FBI has established new units and partnerships to address emerging threats. The Cyber Division is responsible for investigating cybercrime and cyber terrorism, while the Joint Terrorism Task Force works with local law enforcement to prevent and investigate terrorist attacks.

Modern counterintelligence techniques have evolved significantly in recent years, driven in large part by advances in technology and changes in the geopolitical landscape. Here are some of the key techniques used by intelligence agencies today:

Cyber Intelligence: With the growth of the internet and the increasing reliance on digital devices, cyber intelligence has become a critical component of counterintelligence. This involves monitoring and analyzing digital communication networks and systems to identify potential threats and vulnerabilities.

Human Intelligence: Human intelligence, or HUMINT, remains an important tool in counterintelligence. This involves recruiting and managing agents who can gather information and provide insights into the activities of potential adversaries.

Surveillance: Surveillance is another key technique used by counterintelligence agencies. This can involve physical surveillance, such as tailing a suspect or monitoring their movements, or electronic surveillance, such as wiretapping or intercepting communications.

Data Analytics: The increasing volume of data generated by digital devices and networks has created new opportunities for counterintelligence agencies to use data analytics and machine learning algorithms to identify patterns and detect potential threats.

Psychological Operations: Psychological operations, or PSYOPS, involve using propaganda and other techniques to influence the attitudes and behavior of potential adversaries. This can include disinformation campaigns, psychological warfare, and other methods designed to sow confusion and dissent.

Financial Intelligence: Counterintelligence agencies may also use financial intelligence techniques to track the financial activities of potential adversaries. This can involve monitoring financial transactions, identifying illicit funds, and disrupting money laundering networks.

Biometric and Identity Analysis: Biometric and identity analysis techniques, such as facial recognition and fingerprint analysis, can be used to identify potential threats and track the movements of suspects.

As we move into the future, the field of counterintelligence is likely to face new challenges and opportunities. Here are some of the key trends and developments to watch:

Artificial Intelligence: Artificial intelligence and machine learning are likely to play an increasingly important role in counterintelligence, enabling agencies to analyze large volumes of data and identify potential threats more quickly and accurately.

Cyber Threats: Cyber threats are likely to remain a key area of focus for counterintelligence agencies, as cyber criminals and nation-state actors continue to develop new methods of attack and exploitation.

Globalization: The increasing interconnectedness of the global economy and the ease of travel have made it easier for individuals and organizations to move money and goods across borders, creating new challenges for counterintelligence agencies.

Climate Change: Climate change is likely to have significant geopolitical and security implications in the coming decades, potentially creating new sources of conflict and instability that counterintelligence agencies will need to address.

Ethics and Privacy: As the use of technology and data analytics becomes more prevalent in counterintelligence, there are likely to be increasing concerns about ethics and privacy. Agencies will need to balance the need for effective intelligence gathering with the protection of individual rights and freedoms.

The future of counterintelligence is likely to be shaped by a combination of technological, geopolitical, and ethical factors. Agencies will need to be agile and adaptable, and constantly evolve their tactics and strategies to stay ahead of emerging threats.

Chapter 3: Salting

In the previous chapter, we discussed the history and evolution of counterintelligence, from ancient civilizations to modern times. Now, we will dive into the specific techniques used by counterintelligence professionals to protect national security and thwart potential threats.

Over the course of the next several chapters, we will explore a range of counterintelligence skills. Each technique is designed to address a specific aspect of counterintelligence, and can be used in a variety of contexts, from military operations to corporate security.

Moving forward in this chapter, we will begin with Salting, a technique used to detect and identify individuals who may be attempting to infiltrate an organization or operation.

Salting involves deliberately planting false information or materials, such as fake documents or computer files, in order to gauge the level of security within an organization and identify potential vulnerabilities.

Salting is an essential technique in the field of counterintelligence, as it allows agencies to proactively identify and neutralize potential threats before they can cause significant harm. In the following part of this chapter, we will provide a guide to implementing this technique effectively, covering everything from planning and preparation to execution and follow-up.

Whether you are a seasoned counterintelligence professional or new to the field, mastering the art of Salting is a crucial step in protecting national security and safeguarding critical assets. So let's dive in and learn how to use this powerful technique to defend against potential threats.

Before engaging in Salting, it is essential to carefully plan and prepare for the operation. Here are some key steps to follow:

Identify the Target: The first step in planning a Salting operation is to identify the target or targets. This could be an individual or group that you suspect is attempting to infiltrate your organization or operation.

Determine the Objectives: Once you have identified the target, you need to determine the objectives of the Salting operation. What do you hope to achieve? What information do you want to gather? What vulnerabilities do you want to expose?

Choose the Right Materials: The success of a Salting operation depends on the quality of the materials used. Choose materials that are realistic and plausible, but also tailored to the specific target and objectives of the operation.

Establish a Cover Story: In order to plant the materials, you will need a cover story that explains why you have access to them. This could involve creating a fake identity or position within the organization.

Develop a Plan for Planting the Materials: Finally, you need to develop a detailed plan for how you will plant the materials, taking into account factors such as timing, location, and potential risks or complications.

Operational security, or OPSEC, is a crucial aspect to consider during the execution phase of a Salting operation. OPSEC measures aim to ensure that the Salting operation remains undetected and uncompromised by hostile individuals or organizations. To effectively maintain OPSEC, it is essential to consider the following:

Minimize Exposure: Keep the Salting operation as small as possible by limiting the number of individuals who are aware of the operation. Only involve those individuals who are necessary for the success of the mission. For example, if the objective is to detect a mole in a specific department, only individuals within that department should be aware of the operation.

Protect Your Cover Story: Your cover story should be strong and credible enough to withstand scrutiny. Ensure that all aspects of your story are consistent, logical, and have verifiable components. Avoid any behavior that could potentially arouse suspicion and cause people to question your legitimacy. Remember that a strong cover story can help to prevent a potential compromise of the Salting operation.

Monitor the Target: Keep track of the target's movements, activities, and habits during the Salting operation. This will enable you to anticipate any potential risks or complications. Ensure that any communication between team members during the operation is secure and cannot be intercepted or compromised.

Maintain Communication: Communication among team members is critical to the success of a Salting operation. Establish clear and secure lines of communication and ensure that all team members are aware of the plan and any changes that may occur. Any communication related to the Salting operation should be conducted using secure methods such as encrypted messaging apps or secure phone lines.

Clean Up After the Operation: After the Salting operation is complete, it is essential to remove all evidence of the operation. This includes any materials that were planted or used during the operation, any records that may have been created, and any communication that may have been exchanged. The objective is to leave no trace of the Salting operation and prevent any potential compromise or exposure.

By following these guidelines, you can increase your chances of success and minimize the risk of exposure or failure. Remember that operational security is essential during the execution phase of a Salting operation, and every step must be taken to protect the operation from compromise or detection.

Once the Salting operation has been completed, it is crucial to conduct post-operation follow-up and analysis. This phase allows you to assess the effectiveness of the operation, identify any potential risks or vulnerabilities, and make necessary adjustments for future operations.

The following steps should be taken during the post-operation follow-up and analysis:

Collect and Analyze Data: Gather all data and information collected during the operation, including any reports or observations made by team members. Analyze the data to determine the success of the operation and identify any areas for improvement.

Identify Risks and Vulnerabilities: Evaluate any potential risks or vulnerabilities that were identified during the operation. These could include weaknesses in operational security, flaws in the cover story, or any other issues that could have compromised the operation's success.

Conduct Debriefings: Debrief all team members involved in the operation to discuss what worked well, what could have been improved, and any potential risks or vulnerabilities identified during the operation.

Make Necessary Adjustments: Use the information gathered during the post-operation follow-up and analysis to make any necessary adjustments to future operations. This could include changes to the cover story, adjustments to operational security measures, or modifications to the Salting techniques used.

Maintain Records: Keep detailed records of the Salting operation, including any data gathered, observations made, and the results of the post-operation follow-up and analysis. This information can be used to inform future operations and improve the effectiveness of the Salting technique.

By conducting thorough post-operation follow-up and analysis, you can ensure that the Salting operation is effective, efficient, and achieves its objectives. It also allows you to continuously improve your Salting technique, making it more effective and better suited to achieving your objectives in future operations.

Like any counterintelligence technique, Salting is not foolproof, and there are potential pitfalls and challenges that you may encounter during the operation. By being aware of these challenges and planning for them in advance, you can increase the chances of success and minimize the risks.

The following are some potential pitfalls and challenges that you may encounter during a Salting operation:

Exposure: The most significant risk of a Salting operation is exposure. If the target becomes suspicious and discovers the planted information, it could compromise the operation and put your team at risk.

Operational Security: Maintaining operational security is crucial to the success of the Salting operation. Any breaches in operational security, such as loose lips or sloppy tradecraft, could compromise the operation and put your team at risk.

Credibility of the Planted Information: The credibility of the information you plant is crucial. If the information appears to be fabricated or unrealistic, it could raise suspicion and compromise the operation.

Overreliance on the Salting Technique: While Salting can be an effective technique, it should not be overused or relied upon too heavily. Overuse can lead to burnout and desensitization, and may even lead to the target becoming aware of the technique and taking measures to counter it.

Inadequate Resources: Conducting a Salting operation requires significant resources, including time, money, and personnel. Inadequate resources can compromise the success of the operation and put your team at risk.

By being aware of these potential pitfalls and challenges, you can plan for them in advance and take necessary measures to minimize their impact.

Like any counterintelligence technique, Salting raises ethical considerations that must be addressed before conducting the operation. While it can be an effective technique for obtaining valuable information, it also involves deception and potentially compromising the integrity of the information.

The following are some ethical considerations that should be addressed before conducting a Salting operation:

Legality: Before conducting a Salting operation, it is essential to ensure that it is legal and does not violate any laws or regulations.

Integrity of the Information: Planting false information can compromise the integrity of the information and raise ethical concerns. It is important to consider whether the potential benefits of obtaining the information outweigh the risks to the integrity of the information.

Potential Harm: The Salting operation may result in harm to the target or others if the information is acted upon. It is important to consider the potential harm and ensure that it is minimized as much as possible.

Transparency: Counterintelligence operations often involve secrecy and deception, which can raise ethical concerns. It is important to consider how transparent the operation should be and to ensure that appropriate stakeholders are aware of the operation.

Consequences: It is important to consider the potential consequences of the Salting operation, both for the target and for the larger organization. It is essential to ensure that the potential benefits of the operation outweigh the potential harm.

By addressing these ethical considerations and ensuring that the operation is conducted in a lawful and ethical manner, you can minimize the risks and maximize the benefits of the Salting operation.

Chapter 4: Crafting a Backstop

Chapter 4: Crafting a Backstop

A critical element of successful counterintelligence operations is the use of backstops. A backstop is a fictitious identity or persona used to create a plausible cover story for a case officer or asset. It serves as a protective measure in case an individual is caught and questioned by the adversary. By providing a plausible and consistent explanation for the individual's activities, the backstop can prevent the adversary from uncovering the true nature of the operation.

In this chapter, we will discuss the process of crafting a backstop, including selecting an appropriate cover story, creating supporting documentation, and maintaining the backstop over time.

What is a Backstop?

A backstop is a critical element of any counterintelligence operation. It is a fictitious identity or persona that serves as a cover story for a case officer or asset. The backstop is designed to create a plausible and consistent explanation for the individual's activities, should they be questioned or caught by the adversary.

A backstop typically includes a name, job title, employment history, and personal background information. It may also include supporting documentation, such as a fake passport or identification card, to lend credibility to the cover story. The goal is to create a backstop that is believable and consistent with the individual's background and skills, while also supporting the goals of the operation.

Creating an effective backstop requires careful planning and attention to detail. It is essential to select an appropriate cover story, create supporting documentation, and maintain the backstop over time. By doing so, you can ensure that your operation remains protected and that your assets are able to operate effectively in the face of potential threats.

Before crafting a backstop, it is essential to identify the objectives of the operation. This will help you to create a cover story that is consistent with the goals of the operation and that will provide a plausible explanation for the individual's activities.

To identify the objectives of the backstop, consider the following questions:

What is the overall goal of the operation?

What specific activities will the individual be engaging in?

What risks are associated with the individual's activities?

What is the likelihood that the individual will be questioned or caught by the adversary?

What are the potential consequences if the individual is caught?

By answering these questions, you can begin to identify the objectives of the backstop and develop a cover story that will support those objectives. For example, if the goal of the operation is to gather intelligence on a foreign government, the backstop might involve creating a cover story for a business executive or academic who is conducting research in the country. The cover story might include details about the individual's background and expertise, as well as supporting documentation such as a fake business card or university ID.

By identifying the objectives of the backstop, you can create a cover story that is tailored to the specific needs of the operation and that will provide a plausible explanation for the individual's activities.

Once you have identified the objectives of the backstop, the next step is to select an appropriate cover story for the individual. This involves creating a fictional persona that is consistent with the individual's background and skills, while also supporting the goals of the operation.

To select an appropriate cover story, consider the following factors:

The individual's background and skills: The cover story should be consistent with the individual's background and skills. For example, if the individual has experience in engineering, the cover story might involve working for a company that manufactures industrial equipment.

The objectives of the operation: The cover story should support the objectives of the operation. For example, if the goal of the operation is to gather intelligence on a foreign government, the cover story might involve conducting research for a university or think tank.

The potential risks: The cover story should take into account the potential risks associated with the individual's activities. For example, if the individual is operating in a high-risk environment, the cover story might involve working for a non-governmental organization (NGO) that provides humanitarian aid.

The plausibility of the story: The cover story should be believable and consistent with the individual's background and skills. It should also be able to withstand scrutiny if the individual is questioned or investigated.

By selecting an appropriate cover story, you can create a backstop that is believable and consistent with the individual's background and skills, while also supporting the objectives of the operation.

Creating a legend is a critical step in crafting a backstop. A well-crafted legend can provide the necessary depth and detail to make the cover story believable and convincing. Here are some additional steps to consider when creating a legend:

Develop a detailed backstory: A legend should provide a detailed and consistent backstory for the individual. This can include information about their education, work experience, personal interests, and relationships. The backstory should be tailored to the cover story and be consistent with the individual's background and skills.

Create supporting documentation: In addition to the backstory, supporting documentation can help bolster the legend. This can include fake IDs, business cards, resumes, and references. All documents should be consistent with the legend and the cover story.

Establish a digital presence: A digital presence can also be helpful in creating a believable legend. This can include creating social media profiles, a personal website, or other online content that supports the cover story and provides additional details about the individual's background.

Conduct rehearsals: Before the individual is deployed, it's important to conduct rehearsals to ensure that they are comfortable with their legend and can answer questions convincingly. This can include role-playing scenarios where the individual is asked about their background or job responsibilities.

Continuously update and maintain the legend: Once the individual is deployed, it's important to continuously update and maintain the legend. This can involve creating new supporting documentation or digital content, as well as adjusting the legend to account for new information or changes in the individual's situation.

By following these steps, you can create a detailed and convincing legend that supports the cover story and makes it more difficult for the adversary to unravel.

Once the backstop has been crafted, it's time to implement it. Here are some steps to consider when implementing a backstop:

Test the cover story: Before the individual is deployed, it's important to test the cover story to ensure that it is believable and can withstand scrutiny. This can involve conducting mock interviews or simulations to see how the individual responds to questions about their background or job responsibilities.

Maintain consistency: Once the individual is deployed, it's important to maintain consistency with the cover story and the legend. This includes being mindful of any information that is shared or actions that are taken that may conflict with the cover story.

Document everything: It's important to document all interactions and information obtained during the operation. This includes taking notes during meetings or conversations, and keeping a record of any documents or materials obtained.

Maintain communication: Regular communication with the individual is important to ensure that the backstop is working effectively and to address any issues that may arise. This can include regular check-ins or debriefings to discuss any challenges or concerns.

Continuously update and refine the backstop: As the operation progresses, it's important to continuously update and refine the backstop to account for new information or changes in the situation. This can involve creating new supporting documentation, adjusting the cover story, or even creating a new backstop altogether.

By implementing these steps, you can ensure that the backstop is effective and supports the success of the operation. It's important to remember that crafting and implementing a backstop is a complex process that requires attention to detail and a thorough understanding of the individual and the operation.

Chapter 5: Detecting Deception

Before diving into techniques for detecting deception, it's important to understand what deception is and how it works. Deception is a deliberate attempt to create a false belief or impression in another person's mind. The goal of deception is to manipulate the target's thoughts, feelings, or behaviors in a way that benefits the deceiver.

Deception can take many forms, including lying, concealing information, and exaggerating or minimizing the truth. It can be used in a variety of settings, from interpersonal relationships to business negotiations to political campaigns.

Deception is often accompanied by signs of stress and anxiety in the deceiver, as they are typically trying to hide something or protect themselves from being caught. These signs can manifest themselves in physical behaviors, such as fidgeting or avoiding eye contact, as well as verbal cues, such as stuttering or using vague language.

By understanding the nature of deception, you can begin to develop a framework for detecting it in others. In the following sections, we'll explore some specific techniques and strategies for identifying deception and assessing the veracity of information.

One of the most common ways to detect deception is by observing a person's body language. When people are lying or concealing information, they often display signs of stress and anxiety in their physical behaviors. These signs can be subtle, but with practice, you can learn to recognize them.

Here are some common body language cues to look for when trying to detect deception:

Facial expressions: The face is one of the most expressive parts of the body, and it can reveal a lot about a person's emotional state. Look for micro-expressions, such as a brief flash of fear or anger, that may indicate that the person is hiding something.

Eye contact: When people are lying, they often avoid eye contact, either by looking away or staring too intently. However, some people may try to overcompensate by staring too long, which can also be a sign of deception.

Posture: A person's posture can reveal a lot about their emotional state. When people are anxious or stressed, they may hunch their shoulders or fidget with their hands. Alternatively, they may try to appear more confident by standing up straight or puffing out their chest.

Gestures: When people are lying, they may use exaggerated gestures or perform unnecessary movements to distract from their deception. They may also perform fewer gestures than usual, as they are focused on maintaining their false narrative.

Speech patterns: Changes in a person's speech patterns, such as hesitations, pauses, or stutters, can be a sign of deception. They may also use more filler words, such as "um" or "ah," to buy themselves time to think of a lie.

In order to detect deception, it is important to establish baselines of the subject's behavior and communication patterns. A baseline is the normal behavior and communication style of the person being observed, and it is established through observation over a period of time. Once the baseline is established, any changes in behavior or communication can be a sign of deception.

To establish a baseline, an observer should begin by observing the subject in a non-threatening situation. This can be done by engaging the subject in casual conversation, asking simple questions, or observing the subject's behavior in a natural setting. The observer should take note of the subject's tone of voice, body language, and any other observable behaviors.

It is important to note that establishing a baseline can take time and may require multiple observations. It is also important to consider the context of the situation and the subject's cultural background, as this can impact their behavior and communication style.

Once the baseline is established, any deviations from it can be a sign of deception. For example, if the subject is normally talkative and outgoing but becomes quiet and withdrawn when asked about a certain topic, this may be a sign of deception.

Deception detection involves the analysis of both verbal and non-verbal cues. Verbal cues can include changes in the subject's tone of voice, pitch, and rate of speech. For example, if the subject's voice becomes higher or lower than their normal speaking voice, it could be a sign of deception. Non-verbal cues can include changes in facial expressions, body language, and gestures.

Some common non-verbal cues associated with deception include avoiding eye contact, fidgeting, and the use of hand-to-face movements, such as rubbing the nose or mouth. These behaviors can indicate nervousness or anxiety, which may be associated with deception.

It is important to note that these cues should not be interpreted in isolation, but rather in conjunction with other verbal and non-verbal behaviors. For example, if the subject avoids eye contact while also exhibiting a change in tone of voice, it may be a stronger indication of deception.

In addition, it is important to consider the context of the situation and the individual's cultural background when interpreting verbal and non-verbal cues. Some cultures may exhibit different non-verbal behaviors that are not necessarily associated with deception.

A key aspect of deception detection is establishing a baseline for the subject's normal behavior. This involves observing the subject's typical patterns of behavior, communication style, and mannerisms, and noting any deviations from this baseline during subsequent interactions.

For example, if the subject normally maintains eye contact during conversation but avoids it during a specific interaction, it could indicate that they are being deceptive. Similarly, if the subject typically speaks in a steady tone but becomes agitated or defensive during a particular conversation, it could be a sign of deception.

Establishing a baseline for the subject's behavior can be accomplished through a variety of means, such as conducting initial interviews or observing the subject in a non-threatening setting. This baseline analysis can then be used as a reference point for subsequent interactions, allowing for more accurate detection of potential deception.

It is important to note that baseline analysis is not foolproof and should be used in conjunction with other techniques and methods for detecting deception. It is also important to consider the individual's personality, culture, and other contextual factors that may influence their behavior and communication style.

Microexpressions are subtle, involuntary facial expressions that can last for a fraction of a second. These brief expressions can reveal a person's true emotions, even if they are attempting to conceal them. In the context of deception detection, microexpressions can provide clues to a person's underlying emotions and intentions.

Examples of microexpressions include a fleeting frown, a brief flash of anger or surprise, or a momentary look of fear or disgust. These expressions can be difficult to detect and interpret, but with training, they can be a valuable tool for identifying potential deception.

One approach to detecting microexpressions is to use a tool called a microexpression training tool (METT). This tool involves studying images of different microexpressions and practicing recognizing them in real-time situations.

It Is important to note that microexpressions should not be relied on as the sole method for detecting deception. They should be used in conjunction with other techniques, such as baseline analysis and verbal cues, to build a more comprehensive understanding of the subject's behavior and intentions.

Statement analysis is a technique that involves examining a person's spoken or written statements for linguistic cues that may reveal deception. This technique is based on the idea that deceptive statements may contain certain patterns or structures that differ from truthful statements.

Some examples of linguistic cues that may indicate deception include the use of vague language, a lack of details or specifics, contradictions within the statement, and an excessive use of pronouns. These cues can be identified by analyzing the subject's language and comparing it to their baseline communication patterns.

One approach to statement analysis is to use a tool called the Scientific Content Analysis (SCAN). This tool involves analyzing the subject's statement word-by-word and sentence-by-sentence to identify inconsistencies and other linguistic cues that may indicate deception.

It Is important to note that statement analysis should be used in conjunction with other techniques, such as microexpressions and body language analysis, to build a more comprehensive understanding of the subject's behavior and intentions. Additionally, it is important to consider cultural and linguistic differences when analyzing statements from individuals who come from different backgrounds or speak different languages.

Chapter 6: Bread Crumbs

The Breadcrumbs Technique is a method used in counterintelligence to trace the source of leaked or stolen information. This technique involves the deliberate inclusion of false or unique pieces of information in a document or communication, which can be used to identify the recipient who leaked or stole the information. The technique is effective in exposing moles or spies, and it can also be used to deter potential leakers or spies by creating a sense of uncertainty and mistrust.

Part 1: Creating the Breadcrumbs

The first step in using the Breadcrumbs Technique is to create the breadcrumbs. This involves including unique pieces of information in the document or communication that can be used to identify the recipient. The information should be plausible and appear to be a part of the overall message, but it should also be distinct enough to be easily identified. The information should be tailored to the specific recipient or group of recipients to increase the chances of identifying the source of the leak.

One common way to create breadcrumbs is to use a specific font, formatting, or style that is unique to the recipient. For example, if the recipient works in a specific department or uses a particular software program, the document can be formatted to match the style or font used in that department or software program. Another way to create breadcrumbs is to use specific language or terminology that is unique to the recipient, such as jargon or slang.

It Is important to note that the breadcrumbs should be created in a way that does not raise suspicion or draw attention to the fact that they are unique. If the breadcrumbs are too obvious, the recipient may realize that they are being tracked and take steps to cover their tracks. Therefore, it is important to be subtle and to create breadcrumbs that blend in with the overall message.

The next step is to distribute the document or communication and monitor its distribution to identify the recipient who leaked or stole the information.

The second step In using the breadcrumbs technique is to determine the specific information that you want to extract from the target. This information should be relevant to your investigation and help you achieve your goals. It is important to approach this step with a clear understanding of your objectives and the information that is necessary to achieve them. For example, if you are investigating a potential leak of sensitive information, you may want to focus on identifying the source of the leak and any individuals who may have been involved in its dissemination.

Once you have identified the information that you want to extract, you should begin to identify potential sources of this information. These sources may include individuals who are directly involved in the situation, as well as those who may have indirect knowledge or access to the information. It is important to cast a wide net and consider all possible sources of information, even those that may seem unlikely or difficult to access.

Once you have identified potential sources of information, you should begin to collect breadcrumbs from each of these sources. This may involve conducting interviews, reviewing documents or correspondence, or observing the behaviors of individuals who may be involved. The key is to remain vigilant and open-minded, collecting any and all information that may help you to piece together the larger puzzle.

In order to effectively collect breadcrumbs, it is important to remain focused and methodical in your approach. This means taking detailed notes, recording conversations where possible, and organizing your findings in a clear and logical manner. It may also involve using specialized tools or software to help you manage and analyze the data that you collect.

By carefully and systematically collecting breadcrumbs from a variety of sources, you can begin to build a more complete picture of the situation that you are investigating. This can help you to identify patterns, connections, and potential leads that may help you to achieve your objectives. However, it is important to approach this process with caution, always remaining mindful of the potential for false leads or incomplete information.

Once you have identified the information you want to leak, you must then find a way to make it public without raising suspicion. This is where the breadcrumbs technique comes in. The goal of the breadcrumbs technique is to make it seem like the information was accidentally leaked or disclosed, rather than intentionally given away. By doing so, it decreases the likelihood that anyone will suspect foul play or question the authenticity of the information.

To start, you should create a trail of seemingly unrelated breadcrumbs that lead to the information you want to disclose. These breadcrumbs can be small pieces of information, rumors, or even fake news stories. The key is to make them believable and realistic enough that people will start to put the pieces together.

For example, if you wanted to leak information about a new product launch, you could start by planting a rumor about a new hire in the marketing department. Then, you could leak a small detail about the new product in an unrelated conversation. Finally, you could send an anonymous tip to a reporter about the upcoming launch, making it seem like a well-intentioned leak.

It's Important to note that the breadcrumbs should be spread out over time, so as not to raise suspicion. If you were to leak all the information at once, it would be much more obvious that it was intentionally leaked. By spreading it out over time, you create the illusion that the information is coming from different sources, making it more difficult to trace back to you.

Once you have identified the information you want to leak, you must then find a way to make it public without raising suspicion. This is where the breadcrumbs technique comes in. The goal of the breadcrumbs technique is to make it seem like the information was accidentally leaked or disclosed, rather than intentionally given away. By doing so, it decreases the likelihood that anyone will suspect foul play or question the authenticity of the information.

To start, you should create a trail of seemingly unrelated breadcrumbs that lead to the information you want to disclose.

These breadcrumbs can be small pieces of information, rumors, or even fake news stories. The key is to make them believable and realistic enough that people will start to put the pieces together.

For example, if you wanted to leak information about a new product launch, you could start by planting a rumor about a new hire in the marketing department. Then, you could leak a small detail about the new product in an unrelated conversation. Finally, you could send an anonymous tip to a reporter about the upcoming launch, making it seem like a well-intentioned leak.

It's Important to note that the breadcrumbs should be spread out over time, so as not to raise suspicion. If you were to leak all the information at once, it would be much more obvious that it was intentionally leaked. By spreading it out over time, you create the illusion that the information is coming from different sources, making it more difficult to trace back to you.

The next step In the breadcrumbs technique is to start monitoring the individual's online activity. This includes social media platforms, online forums, and any other digital platforms the individual might use. This monitoring should be done carefully, without tipping off the individual that they are being watched.

During this phase, it is important to look for any patterns or trends in the individual's online activity. This could include changes in the types of websites they visit, the times of day they are most active online, or changes in the content they are posting or commenting on.

It is also important to pay attention to the language the individual uses in their online communications. This can provide valuable insight into their mindset, personality, and potential motives. Are they using certain buzzwords or phrases? Are they expressing extreme views or opinions? All of these factors can help build a more complete picture of the individual's behavior and intentions.

The key to making the breadcrumbs technique work effectively is to make the trail of breadcrumbs seem natural and not contrived. This requires a great deal of planning and attention to detail. For example, you might start by creating a fake identity or persona that appears to be a genuine individual. You would need to create social media profiles, email addresses, and other online accounts that are all tied to this persona.

Once you have established this fake identity, you can start to create breadcrumbs that lead to it. For example, you might leave comments on social media posts that are related to your field of interest or expertise, using your fake identity. You might also create blog posts or other content under your fake identity that appear to be genuine contributions to the field.

As you begin to create this trail of breadcrumbs, it's important to be mindful of how you are doing so. You want to avoid making it too obvious that you are intentionally leaving a trail. Instead, the breadcrumbs should appear to be the natural result of your interests and activities in the field.

In addition to creating a trail of breadcrumbs that leads to your fake identity, you should also take steps to make your fake identity appear more legitimate. This might include creating a LinkedIn profile that looks like it belongs to a real person, complete with a work history and recommendations from colleagues.

Ultimately, the goal of the breadcrumbs technique is to create a trail that leads an adversary to a false conclusion. By leading them down a path that appears to be genuine and legitimate, you can create a false sense of confidence in their own analysis, while simultaneously hiding your true intentions and activities. However, it's important to remember that this technique requires a great deal of planning and attention to detail, and can be difficult to pull off effectively.

Chapter 7: Canary Trap

The canary trap technique is a type of counterintelligence method that involves leaving different versions of the same sensitive information with different individuals or groups, in order to identify potential leaks or sources of compromise. The idea behind the canary trap is that if any of the versions of the information is leaked, the investigator can trace it back to the individual or group that received that specific version.

The technique Is also referred to as the "barium meal" or "test word" technique. The former term comes from the medical practice of using barium to highlight specific areas of the digestive system for diagnostic purposes, while the latter refers to the use of a unique word or phrase that is included in each version of the information in order to identify the source of the leak.

The canary trap technique is used in a variety of contexts, including intelligence agencies, corporate environments, and legal investigations. In this chapter, we will explore the history of the technique, its applications, and the steps involved in its implementation.

The origins of the canary trap technique can be traced back to the world of espionage, where intelligence agencies have long used various methods to protect their classified information. One of the earliest recorded instances of the technique can be found in the book "Operation Solo: The FBI's Man in the Kremlin," which chronicles the life of Morris Childs, a key figure in the Communist Party USA who became a secret informant for the FBI. As part of his cooperation, Childs provided the FBI with different versions of his reports, each containing a unique identifier, which helped the agency to identify leaks and monitor the effectiveness of its intelligence gathering.

Since then, the canary trap technique has been adopted by various other agencies, including the CIA and MI6, as well as by private companies and legal teams. It has also been used in high-profile cases, such as the investigation into the leak of the identity of CIA operative Valerie Plame.

The canary trap technique can be used in a variety of settings and scenarios. One of its primary applications is in the field of intelligence gathering, where agencies use it to identify potential moles or traitors who may be passing information to foreign governments or other organizations. It can also be used in the corporate world, where companies may use it to identify employees who are leaking sensitive information to competitors or other parties.

Legal teams may also use the canary trap technique in litigation cases, where the authenticity of documents or testimony may be in question. By including a unique identifier in different versions of the information, they can help to establish the source of the leak or the veracity of the testimony.

Implementing the canary trap technique requires careful planning and attention to detail. The following are the key steps involved in the process:

Identify the sensitive information: The first step in implementing the canary trap technique is to identify the information that needs to be protected. This could be classified intelligence, confidential business plans, or sensitive legal documents.

Create multiple versions of the information: Once the sensitive information has been identified, the next step is to create multiple versions of it, each containing a unique identifier. The identifier could be a particular word or phrase, a specific formatting style, or even a small change in the content.

Distribute the versions: The different versions of the information should then be distributed to different individuals or groups. It is important to ensure that each version is distributed to a specific group or individual, and that the distribution is carefully tracked.

Monitor for leaks: Once the versions have been distributed, the investigator should monitor for any leaks.

Another important aspect of creating a canary trap is to ensure that the bait material is authentic and contains unique identifiable markers. The markers can include specific words or phrases, typographical errors, or even specific formatting styles. These markers can help in identifying the source of the leak and help the counterintelligence team in taking appropriate action.

The canary trap technique can also be used in a more sophisticated manner with the use of technology. In this case, the bait material can be embedded with digital markers or watermarks. These markers can help in identifying the specific user who leaked the information and even the time and date of the leak. Digital canary traps can also be set up to alert the counterintelligence team in real-time when a leak is detected, allowing them to take immediate action.

One of the key advantages of the canary trap technique is that it does not require any special skills or tools, making it accessible to a wide range of organizations. However, it is important to note that the effectiveness of the technique depends heavily on the authenticity and uniqueness of the bait material. If the material is too generic or widely available, it may not be effective in identifying the source of the leak.

Another potential limitation of the canary trap technique is that it can only detect leaks after they have occurred. This means that the damage may already be done by the time the leak is identified. To address this limitation, organizations can use a combination of different counterintelligence techniques, including proactive monitoring and access control measures, to minimize the risk of leaks in the first place.

Chapter 8: Mail Covers

Mail covers are a common form of postal surveillance used by intelligence agencies and law enforcement agencies around the world. The technique involves intercepting and examining the outside of mail, including envelopes and packages, in order to gather intelligence on the sender and recipient. Mail covers can be a highly effective tool in investigations, but they must be conducted in accordance with the law and with the utmost care to avoid violating the privacy rights of individuals.

In this chapter, we will provide a comprehensive guide to conducting mail covers. We will cover everything from the legal framework to the practical considerations of implementing a mail cover program. Whether you are a law enforcement officer, intelligence analyst, or simply interested in the topic, this guide will provide you with the knowledge and skills you need to conduct effective mail covers.

Legal Framework

Before conducting a mail cover, it is important to understand the legal framework governing this technique. In the United States, mail covers are governed by Title 18, Section 1702 of the U.S. Code, which allows for the interception and examination of mail for investigative purposes. However, this law requires that the mail cover be authorized by a warrant or court order. In addition, the Postal Service regulations require that mail covers be conducted in accordance with strict procedures and guidelines.

It is important to note that mail covers are not a form of wiretapping or electronic surveillance, and therefore do not fall under the purview of the Foreign Intelligence Surveillance Act (FISA). However, there are still strict rules and regulations that must be followed to ensure that mail covers are conducted in a legal and ethical manner.

Once you have obtained the necessary legal authorization to conduct a mail cover, it is important to carefully plan and implement the program. The first step is to identify the target mail stream that you wish to cover. This could be a specific mail route, a particular post office, or even a single mailbox.

Once you have identified the target mail stream, the next step is to develop a plan for intercepting and examining the mail. This may involve working with postal employees to identify and flag the mail, or it may involve physically intercepting and examining the mail as it passes through a particular point.

It Is important to note that mail covers are not an open-ended surveillance technique. They are typically authorized for a specific period of time, and only for the purpose of gathering specific information related to an investigation. Therefore, it is important to carefully define the scope and duration of the mail cover, and to ensure that the program is conducted in accordance with the authorization and legal guidelines.

Practical Considerations

There are a number of practical considerations to keep in mind when conducting a mail cover. One of the most important is the need to maintain strict chain of custody procedures to ensure that the mail is not tampered with or compromised in any way.

Another important consideration is the need for clear and concise documentation of the mail cover program. This documentation should include details such as the target mail stream, the scope and duration of the program, and the specific information that is being gathered.

In addition, it is important to consider the potential impact of the mail cover on the individuals whose mail is being intercepted and examined. This can include the need to redact or protect sensitive personal information, as well as the need to ensure that the mail is not damaged or delayed in any way.

In addition to monitoring outgoing mail, mail covers can also be used to track incoming mail. In these cases, law enforcement officials may place a mail cover on the addressee's mailbox, rather than on the outgoing mail. The mail carrier then informs law enforcement of any mail that is received at that address, and the contents of the mail can be inspected and recorded as part of an investigation.

It Is worth noting that the use of mail covers is controversial, as some argue that it constitutes an invasion of privacy. Others argue that mail covers are a necessary tool for law enforcement agencies in order to prevent criminal activity and ensure public safety.

Despite the controversy, mail covers remain a powerful tool for counterintelligence and law enforcement agencies, and are likely to continue to be used in the future. As technology continues to advance and new forms of communication emerge, it will be interesting to see how the use of mail covers evolves in response.

Chapter 9:

Creating a fake social media footprint is a common technique used in the world of counterintelligence. By creating a seemingly legitimate online persona, an individual or organization can use this fake profile to gather information, manipulate others, or conduct covert operations. In this chapter, we will explore the various steps and strategies for creating a convincing fake social media footprint.

Step 1: Determine Your Objective

The first step in creating a fake social media footprint is to determine your objective. What are you trying to achieve by creating this profile? Are you trying to gather information from a particular individual or group? Are you trying to manipulate others for political or financial gain? Or are you simply trying to create a convincing profile for a fictional character?

Once you have determined your objective, you can begin to develop a plan for your fake social media profile. This plan should include details such as the name, age, location, interests, and personality traits of your fake persona.

Step 2: Choose Your Social Media Platform

The next step is to choose the social media platform that you will use for your fake profile. Consider the platform that your target audience uses the most, as this will increase the chances of your fake persona being seen and engaging with others.

Some popular social media platforms to consider include Facebook, Twitter, Instagram, and LinkedIn. Each platform has its own unique features and benefits, so choose the one that aligns with your objectives and target audience.

Step 3: Create Your Profile

Once you have chosen your social media platform, it's time to create your profile. This is where you will bring your fake persona to life. Start by choosing a profile picture that matches the age, gender, and interests of your fake persona. Make sure that the photo is clear and looks like a real person.

Next, fill out your profile information, including your name, age, location, and bio. Make sure that the information you provide is consistent with your fake persona's objective and backstory. For example, if your fake persona is a 25-year-old software developer from California, make sure that your profile information reflects this.

Step 4: Build Your Social Network

The next step is to build your social network. Start by following other users who are in your target audience or who share similar interests with your fake persona. Interact with them by liking, commenting, and sharing their posts. This will help you build credibility and establish your fake persona as a real person.

You can also join groups and communities related to your fake persona's interests. This will give you the opportunity to engage with other users who share those interests and potentially gather information that can be useful for your objective.

Step 5: Maintain Your Profile

Once you have created your fake social media profile and built your social network, it's important to maintain your profile. Post regular updates and engage with your followers to keep your profile active and believable. You can also use automation tools to schedule posts and engage with followers when you're not available.

However, it's important to be careful not to engage in any suspicious or illegal activities that could compromise your fake persona or put you at risk. Remember, the goal of creating a fake social media footprint is to gather information or achieve a specific objective, not to cause harm or engage in illegal activities.

Step 6: Monitor and Adapt

Finally, it's important to monitor your fake social media footprint and adapt your strategy as needed. Keep track of your interactions and engagements with other users, as well as any information or data that you gather. Use this information to refine your strategy and achieve your objectives more effectively.

Chapter 10: Deepfake Detection

Deepfakes are manipulated or altered videos or images that use advanced artificial intelligence techniques to create realistic but false content. They are a growing concern in the digital age as they can be used for malicious purposes such as propaganda, disinformation, and political manipulation. Detecting deepfakes is a difficult challenge as they are often difficult to spot with the naked eye. In order to accurately detect deepfakes, a number of specialized techniques and tools have been developed. These include:

Facial and body movements analysis: One of the key features of deepfake videos is that they often have unnatural facial and body movements. This can include distorted facial expressions, unnatural eye movements, and incorrect head movements. To detect deepfakes, sophisticated algorithms can be used to analyze these movements and identify any anomalies.

Audio analysis: Deepfake videos can also be detected through audio analysis. This can include analyzing the pitch, tone, and other features of the audio to determine if it is genuine or not. Additionally, deepfakes may use artificial speech synthesis techniques to create convincing but fake audio. Analysis of the audio can help detect these synthetic voices.

Metadata analysis: Deepfakes may also contain hidden metadata that can reveal information about their origin or creation. By analyzing the metadata, researchers can identify any discrepancies or inconsistencies that may indicate the video has been manipulated.

Reverse image search: Another technique for detecting deepfakes is to use reverse image search tools to check if any of the content has been taken from other sources. If parts of the video or image can be identified as having been copied from another source, it is likely that the content has been manipulated.

Deep learning algorithms: Advanced deep learning algorithms have been developed to detect deepfakes. These algorithms use machine learning techniques to analyze the content and identify any anomalies or inconsistencies that may indicate the content has been manipulated.

Collaborative detection: Given the increasing sophistication of deepfakes, it is unlikely that any single detection technique will be sufficient. Instead, a collaborative approach that combines multiple detection methods is likely to be more effective. By combining different techniques, researchers can increase the accuracy of their detection methods and reduce the risk of false positives or false negatives.

Forensic Analysis:

Forensic analysis involves looking for subtle digital traces left behind by the deepfake creation process. This approach may involve looking for inconsistencies in the lighting or shadows, differences in the facial expressions, or mismatches in audio quality. Forensic analysis techniques are often used to verify the authenticity of images and videos in legal proceedings, and can be adapted to detect deepfakes as well.

Reverse Engineering:

Another approach to deepfake detection is to reverse engineer the AI model used to create the deepfake. By examining the specific algorithms and techniques used to generate the fake image or video, researchers can develop better ways to identify deepfakes based on the unique features of their creation process.

Multi-Factor Authentication:

Multi-factor authentication involves using a combination of different techniques to verify the authenticity of an image or video. This approach might include looking for telltale signs of a deepfake, comparing the image or video to known real-world data sources, and performing forensic analysis to look for inconsistencies in the image or video itself.

User Education:

Given the rapid pace of deepfake technology, it may be difficult to keep up with the latest detection techniques. As a result, user education is an important component of any deepfake detection strategy. By helping users understand the risks and challenges associated with deepfakes, organizations can reduce the likelihood of individuals being misled by fake images or videos.

Collaboration:

Finally, deepfake detection efforts can be significantly strengthened through collaboration among researchers, technologists, policymakers, and other stakeholders. By sharing knowledge and resources, and by working together to develop new detection techniques, these groups can help mitigate the risks associated with deepfake technology and promote greater trust and transparency in our media environment.

Chapter 11: Elicitation

Elicitation is a process of obtaining information from an individual without them realizing they are providing it. It is a critical skill in counterintelligence, law enforcement, and investigative journalism. Elicitation techniques can be used in various situations, such as interviews, negotiations, and even casual conversations. Skilled elicitors can get people to reveal information that they would not otherwise share, by using subtle psychological techniques that influence human behavior.

The goal of elicitation is to get the subject to reveal information that they would not otherwise disclose. This information can be of significant value to investigators and intelligence analysts, as it can provide critical insights into the subject's behavior, motivations, and intentions. By using elicitation techniques, investigators can gather valuable information without raising suspicion or alerting the subject to their investigation.

In this chapter, we will explore several elicitation techniques that can be used in various settings.

Open-ended questions are an effective way to elicit information from individuals, as they encourage the person to provide a more detailed and descriptive response. These types of questions are designed to start a conversation and allow the individual to share their thoughts and experiences in their own words. Open-ended questions typically begin with words like "what," "how," or "why," and do not have a specific answer.

When using open-ended questions for elicitation, it's important to phrase the question in a way that does not suggest a specific answer or influence the person's response. For example, asking "How did you feel about the project?" is a more open-ended question than "Did you like the project?" which implies a binary "yes" or "no" response.

In addition to avoiding leading questions, it's also important to give the person enough time to respond to the question. Silence can be uncomfortable, but it's important to resist the urge to fill the silence or jump in with another question too quickly. Allowing the person time to gather their thoughts and provide a thoughtful response can lead to more valuable information.

"Playing dumb" is a technique that can be used to elicit information from a target without arousing suspicion. The idea behind this technique is to act as though you do not know much about the topic you are trying to elicit information on, in order to get the target to reveal more information than they otherwise might.

The first step In using this technique is to establish rapport with the target. This can be done by finding common ground, such as shared interests or experiences. Once a rapport has been established, the next step is to begin asking open-ended questions about the topic you are interested in. These questions should be designed to elicit information without giving away that you already know some details.

As the target answers your questions, it is important to continue to play dumb and act surprised or impressed by their responses. This can encourage them to reveal more information or feel more comfortable sharing what they know. It is important to avoid asking too many questions or pushing too hard for information, as this can arouse suspicion and cause the target to become defensive.

Flattery is an effective elicitation technique that is used to build rapport and establish trust with the target. It involves giving compliments and expressing admiration towards the target to lower their guard and make them more open to sharing information.

The technique works by appealing to the target's ego and making them feel good about themselves. By doing so, they may be more likely to disclose information that they might not have otherwise shared. For example, if you are trying to gather information about a company's product roadmap, you could compliment the target on their knowledge of the industry and their expertise in the field. This could lead them to share information about upcoming products or projects that they are working on.

It Is important to use flattery carefully and to make sure that it is genuine. Overdoing it or coming across as insincere can have the opposite effect and make the target more suspicious. Additionally, it is important to ensure that the flattery does not come across as manipulative or exploitative. If the target feels that they are being used, they are likely to become defensive and less forthcoming with information.

Using misleading statements is another elicitation technique that can be effective in extracting information from individuals. This technique involves making statements that are not entirely accurate or are ambiguous in order to provoke a response from the individual.

One way to use misleading statements is to make a statement that is factually incorrect, but that the individual being elicited may believe to be true. For example, if an individual is suspected of stealing company secrets, the elicitor may make a statement suggesting that the company is planning to move to a new location, when in fact there are no such plans. If the individual responds with surprise or interest, this can indicate that they have been involved in activities related to the company's secrets.

Another way to use misleading statements is to make a statement that is technically true, but that the individual may interpret differently than intended. For example, an elicitor may make a statement such as "I heard that some employees are planning to leave the company soon." The statement is technically true, but the individual may interpret it to mean that a specific employee is planning to leave, even if that is not the case. This can lead the individual to reveal information that they may not have otherwise shared.

Using silence can be a powerful elicitation technique when attempting to extract information from someone. This technique involves simply remaining silent after the person has answered a question or made a statement, and waiting for them to fill the awkward silence with additional information.

Silence can be uncomfortable, and many people are tempted to fill the gap by speaking again. In some cases, the person may feel compelled to clarify or expand upon their previous statement, providing additional details or insights that they might not have shared otherwise.

To use this technique effectively, it's important to be patient and not rush to fill the silence yourself. Give the person time to process their thoughts and consider what they want to say next. This can be challenging, as silence can also be uncomfortable for the person using the technique, but it's important to remain calm and focused.

It's also important to note that this technique can be perceived as manipulative or confrontational if used inappropriately. It's important to approach the use of silence in a respectful and non-threatening way, and to use it only when appropriate and necessary to achieve your elicitation goals.

Asking for advice is a powerful elicitation technique that can work wonders in various contexts. When people feel that they have something valuable to offer, they are more likely to open up and share information that they might not have otherwise.

The technique involves approaching someone and asking for their advice on a particular matter. This could be related to their area of expertise, personal experience, or any other topic they may have knowledge about. By framing the request as a solicitation for advice, the person being elicited feels valued and respected for their opinion, which makes them more inclined to share information.

One key advantage of this technique is that it can help the elicitor gain a deeper understanding of the subject matter while simultaneously gathering useful intelligence. For instance, someone could approach an employee of a competitor company and ask for their advice on how to break into the market. The employee may end up divulging information about their company's strategies, challenges, and opportunities that the elicitor can use to their advantage.

It Is essential to approach this technique with a degree of subtlety and tact. Asking too many questions or coming across as too eager can raise suspicion and make the person being elicited less forthcoming with information. Therefore, the elicitor must strike a delicate balance between showing interest and not appearing too intrusive.

Hourglass elicitation is a technique used to elicit information from a source by asking open-ended questions in a specific sequence that starts broad and narrows down to a specific topic, then broadens back out again. The technique is called "hourglass" because the question sequence resembles the shape of an hourglass.

The technique Is effective because it gradually narrows the focus of the conversation to a specific topic, making it easier for the source to provide detailed information. It also helps build rapport with the source, as the conversation starts with broader, more general questions before moving on to more specific ones.

To use the hourglass elicitation technique, start with broad, open-ended questions that are relevant to the topic of interest. For example, if you're trying to learn more about an individual's job, you might start by asking about their industry, company, or role.

Once the source has provided some general information, move on to more specific questions. For example, if the source is discussing their role, you might ask about their specific responsibilities or challenges they face in their work.

After gathering the specific information you need, broaden the conversation again by asking more general questions. This helps to transition the conversation smoothly and maintain a positive rapport with the source.

It's Important to approach the hourglass elicitation technique with a friendly, curious attitude rather than an aggressive or confrontational one. This will help to build rapport and put the source at ease, increasing the likelihood that they will share useful information.

Chapter 12: Conclusion

The field of counterintelligence is a complex and ever-changing landscape, and the techniques and strategies discussed in this book are just the tip of the iceberg. However, by studying and applying the principles and methods outlined in these pages, readers can gain a deep understanding of the importance of counterintelligence and the various tools and tactics that can be used to protect their organizations from external and internal threats.

Whether you are a government official, a business owner, or simply someone interested in learning more about counterintelligence, the insights and knowledge contained in this book can help you develop a more strategic and effective approach to security. By honing your skills in elicitation, surveillance, canary traps, and other key areas of counterintelligence, you can become a more vigilant and proactive defender of your organization, and help safeguard against threats both now and in the future.

Remember, the world of counterintelligence is constantly evolving, and staying ahead of the curve requires ongoing education and training. But armed with the insights and strategies discussed in this book, you can become a more skilled and effective practitioner of counterintelligence, and make a positive impact on your organization and the world around you.